I see a scary face!   I don't see anything!   Squawk!

For Shan-Tong Andre Jean Widmer

Dear Parents, Teachers, and Librarians,

The story of Pandora was told by a Greek writer named Hesiod (HEE-see-ud) over 2,500 years ago in a poem called "Work and Days." Hesiod said that what covered "hope" in the box were "pains and evils." That phrase is too abstract for a children's book, so I discussed with a class of second graders various specific troubles that are in their own "work and days." Their ideas became the trouble bugs in this book. Your children may have more ideas.

  After children become familiar with this story, they can take parts and read it like a play. Please read last the words of the Greek chorus (the birds below), just before you turn the page.

Jean Marzollo

Special thanks to Bill Mayer, professor of Classical Studies at Hunter College, New York City; Dr. Joanne Marien, superintendent of Somers School District in Somers, New York; Shelley Thornton; Irene O'Garden; Claudio Marzollo; models Stephanie Cairl, Billy Erichson, Dan Marzollo, and Dave Marzollo; agent Molly Friedrich; editor Jennifer Hunt; art director Alyssa Morris; copy editor Christine Cuccio; marketing director Bill Boedeker; publicity director Elizabeth Eulberg; publisher David Ford; Patricia Adams; Chris Nowak; Sheila Rauch; Mim Galligan; Lindsey Turner; Nancy Lockspeiser; Mrs. Moneymaker's second grade class at the Forrestal Elementary School in Beacon, New York; and all the kids who helped me test the book at Philipstown NY Summer Fun.

Little, Brown and Company • Time Warner Book Group
1271 Avenue of the Americas, New York, NY 10020
Visit our Web site at www.lb-kids.com

First Edition: September 2006

Library of Congress Cataloging-in-Publication Data

Marzollo, Jean.
 Pandora's box : a Greek myth about the constellations / retold and illustrated by Jean Marzollo.— 1st ed.
p. cm.
  ISBN-13: 978-0-316-74133-0 (hardcover)
  ISBN-10: 0-316-74133-7 (hardcover)
 1. Pandora (Greek mythology)—Juvenile literature. I. Title.
BL820.P23M37 2007
398.20938'02—dc22   2005024475

10 9 8 7 6 5 4 3 2 1

SC

Manufactured in China

The illustrations for this book were painted in watercolor and Chinese ink, then scanned and assembled like a collage in Adobe Photoshop on a Power Mac G4. The text was set in Hadriano Bold and Kid Print, and the display type was set in Galahad.

The ancient Greeks told great stories and drew pictures of them on vases.   What does "ancient" mean?   Long, long ago.

A GREEK MYTH
Retold and Illustrated by JEAN MARZOLLO

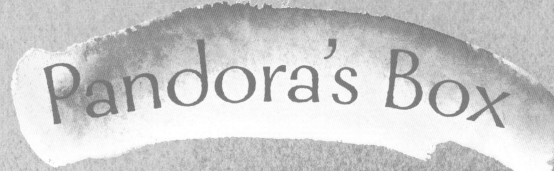

LJB
1837

LITTLE, BROWN AND COMPANY
New York ❧ Boston ❧ London

Are we in this story?   Yes, we're the Greek chorus!   What's that?   We look, we listen, we discuss.   *Squawk!*

Only the Greek gods had fire. Prometheus (Pro-MEE-thee-us)
thought this was unfair. One night, when he was cold,
he climbed to the top of Mount Olympus, where
the gods lived. Quietly, he stole a
torch of fire from the gods.

Prometheus carried the fire carefully down the mountain. By the time he reached the bottom, he was hungry. He was also a little scared because he knew that Zeus, king of the gods, would be mad at him for stealing fire. Still, Prometheus was glad he had done it, for now he could make a warm fire and cook hot cereal. Wouldn't his brother be surprised?

Why will his brother be surprised?   It will be his first hot breakfast ever!   Squawk!

His brother Epimetheus (Ep-uh-MEE-thee-us)
was very surprised, indeed. He loved
his breakfast! In fact, he couldn't
stop talking and eating and
talking and eating.

Tell me again, Prometheus!
How did you steal this wonderful
warm, cozy fire? And how did you
make this yummy cereal?
What do you call it?

Oatmeal. Now, please! Stop talking and listen! I'm sure that King Zeus is watching us from the clouds around Mount Olympus. He will be mad, and he will punish us for having fire. So, be careful! Whatever you do, don't accept any presents from Zeus!

You bet I'm mad!

Why can't Epimetheus accept a present from Zeus?   The present could be a tricky punishment.   Squawk!

King Zeus was famous for tricky
punishments, and he wanted
to make this a good one.

Hm-m. This is a challenge.
Let's see, I need to punish Prometheus
because he stole fire! The nerve of him!
But then, what about Epimetheus? He's going
to use my fire every day to make oatmeal!
What about all the people in the world?
They're going to use my fire, so they
need to be punished, too. Hm-m.
How can I punish everyone?

Now for STEP 2: Zeus waited until Epimetheus was alone. Then, he asked Hermes, the messenger god, to fly Pandora down the mountain and give her in marriage to Epimetheus.

Epimetheus was thrilled.

Wow! King Zeus sent her to me? What a great present! Please tell Zeus thank you!

Didn't Prometheus warn his brother not to accept any gifts from Zeus?   Yes, but Epimetheus forgot.   Uh-oh.   *Squawk!*

Now for STEP 3: Zeus gave Epimetheus and Pandora
a gigantic, magnificent wedding present.

I had this special box made just
for you. It's strong enough
to sit on, but don't
open it. Okay?
Promise?
(Heh, heh, heh.)

Thank you for your wonderful gift! It's fascinating!

Okay, King Zeus! Sure enough! We promise! Wow!

Once again, Epimetheus accepted a gift from Zeus! He keeps forgetting. Squawk!

Pandora and Epimetheus set
the box in their garden.
Days went by.

I'll always remember
the moment when
King Zeus gave us this
fabulous box to sit on.

It's very beautiful, Epimetheus, but don't you wonder what's inside? I'm so curious! Maybe someday we could open it.

Epimetheus isn't curious.   No, but Pandora is.   She wants to know what's inside the box!   *Squawk!*

One day, when Epimetheus went for a walk, Pandora stayed home and examined the box.

Do I hear something inside?

Is there a crack somewhere that I can peek through?

Pandora's going to break it open!   Maybe that's what she wants.   Squawk!

When Pandora knelt down
and touched the lid,
her curiosity got
the best
of her.

I'll just take a
quick peek!

Show-off Bug

Teasy Bug

Greedy Bug

Grabby Bug

Hooray!
Pandora let us out!
Now we can
bug people!

Worry Bug

Loudmouth Bug

Two-Faced Bug

Destruction
Bug

Before this, people weren't bugged by these trouble bugs?   Right. The trouble bugs were Zeus's punishment.   *Squawk!*

Through her tears, Pandora saw something beautiful in the box. It was HOPE! The trouble bugs were trying to grab it.

Pandora slammed
the lid down, as
fast as she
could!

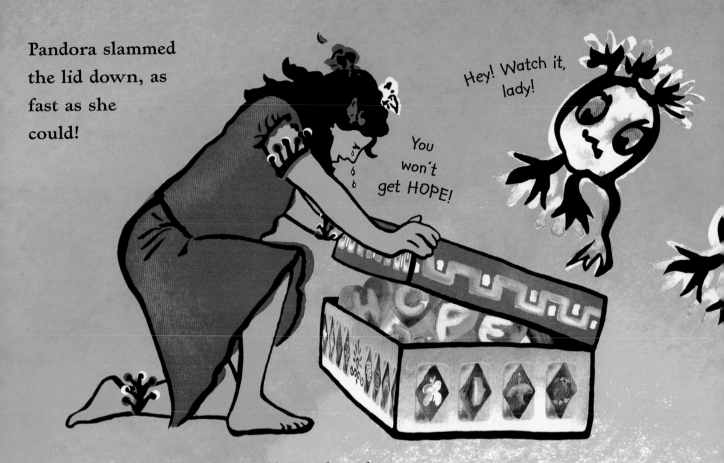

As the trouble bugs flew off, Pandora knew
she had done at least one thing right.
She had saved
HOPE.

Why didn't the *bugs* destroy HOPE before, when they were all inside the box?   Good question. What do you think?   *Squawk!*

So now people on Earth had troubles, but you know what?
They were still glad that Prometheus had stolen fire from the gods.
They even learned to cook more than oatmeal! Sometimes, though,
Pandora was bugged by the Worry Bug.

Do you think people will always remember me as the person who let the trouble bugs out of the box?

I hope that people will remember you more kindly.

I stole fire from the gods and thus
brought punishment to people. But you, Pandora,
you saved hope. Because of you, people
carry hope in their hearts, where
it will always be safe.

 Is Zeus still mad at Prometheus for stealing fire? Is he mad at Pandora for saving hope? *Squawk!*

King Zeus didn't stay mad. Actually, he never was THAT mad at people. After all, he put hope in the box, didn't he? And he gave Pandora curiosity, didn't he? And he let people keep fire, didn't he? Maybe everything that happened was part of his plan.

Fire is nice, but people have to be careful with it.   Same with curiosity.

What do you mean?   Think about it. . . .   Squawk!

(yawning) Some days I feel like I've been bugged by the Lazy Bug.